The AI Gold Rush

The AI Gold Rush

Matthew Petchinsky

1

The AI Gold Rush: How to Profit from the AI Revolution
By: Matthew Petchinsky

Introduction: The AI Industry is Booming—This Guide Shows How to Capitalize on It

Artificial Intelligence (AI) is no longer a futuristic concept—it is here, transforming industries, reshaping economies, and creating unprecedented opportunities for those who recognize its potential. The AI revolution is often compared to historical gold rushes, where those who took decisive action early on reaped the greatest rewards. Whether you're an entrepreneur, investor, content creator, or someone simply looking for ways to future-proof your career, the AI boom presents a unique chance to build wealth, expand businesses, and stay ahead of the technological curve.

In recent years, AI has evolved from a niche scientific pursuit into a mainstream technological force. It powers everything from chatbots and automation tools to content generation, advanced data analytics, and even creative industries like art and music. Companies are racing to integrate AI into their operations, and governments are investing heavily in AI development. This rapid expansion means that AI is not just a trend—it is an economic shift that will define the next era of technological advancement.

Why AI is the New Gold Rush

Just as the internet revolutionized commerce and communication, AI is revolutionizing productivity, efficiency, and decision-making. The global AI market, which was valued at around $150 billion in 2023, is expected to reach trillions of dollars in the coming years. Companies that leverage AI effectively are already seeing exponential growth, while new AI-driven startups are emerging at an unprecedented rate. Those who understand how to harness AI—whether through developing new tools, investing in AI-driven companies, or utilizing AI for business automation—stand to gain immensely.

The key to profiting from this revolution is recognizing AI's potential applications and positioning yourself in the right markets before they become saturated. AI is creating wealth in multiple industries, from healthcare and finance to e-commerce, marketing, and creative fields. Businesses that implement AI-powered automation are cutting costs while increasing efficiency. Freelancers and content creators are using AI to scale their work and generate passive income. Investors are pouring money into AI startups, betting on the next big breakthrough.

Who This Guide is For

This book is designed for anyone looking to capitalize on the AI boom. Whether you are a:

- **Entrepreneur** seeking to launch an AI-driven business or integrate AI into your existing company
- **Investor** interested in identifying high-growth AI stocks, startups, or blockchain-based AI ventures
- **Freelancer or digital creator** looking to automate tasks and increase productivity
- **Employee or job seeker** who wants to future-proof their career by learning AI skills
- **Tech enthusiast** eager to understand the landscape of AI opportunities and trends

This guide provides practical strategies for leveraging AI, regardless of your experience level. You don't need to be a programmer or data scientist to profit from AI—many of the most lucrative AI opportunities require no technical expertise at all. Instead, success comes from knowing where AI is heading and positioning yourself to take advantage of it.

What You'll Learn in This Guide

In *The AI Gold Rush: How to Profit from the AI Revolution*, we break down:

- The most profitable AI-driven industries and business models
- How to leverage AI tools to automate work and scale your income
- Investment opportunities in AI stocks, startups, and blockchain-based AI projects
- How AI is changing the workforce and which skills will be in demand
- The ethics and risks of AI adoption, and how to navigate them

This guide will give you a clear roadmap to making money with AI, from passive income streams to launching an AI-powered business. It will provide real-world examples, case studies, and step-by-step instructions to help you take action immediately.

Why You Should Act Now

We are in the early stages of the AI revolution, and history has shown that those who recognize transformative technologies early reap the greatest rewards. Think of the early days of the internet—those who built websites, started e-commerce stores, or invested in companies like Amazon and Google in the late 1990s are now among the wealthiest people in the world. The AI boom offers a similar once-in-a-generation opportunity.

But as with any gold rush, the window of opportunity won't remain open forever. As AI adoption increases, markets will become saturated, competition will rise, and early adopters will have a significant advantage. The best time to start is now.

Final Thoughts

The AI revolution is here, and it is reshaping the world at an astonishing pace. Whether you are looking for financial freedom, business success, or a way to future-proof your career, AI presents one of the greatest wealth-building opportunities of our time.

This book is your guide to navigating this new frontier and securing your place in the AI-driven future. The tools, strategies, and insights within these pages will help you seize the moment and take advantage of the AI gold rush.

Are you ready to capitalize on the biggest technological shift of our generation? Let's begin.

Chapter 1: Understanding the AI Boom: Why It's Happening Now

Artificial Intelligence (AI) has long been a topic of science fiction, but today, it is one of the most transformative technologies shaping our world. From automating tasks and analyzing massive amounts of data to generating human-like text and creating digital art, AI is revolutionizing industries at an unprecedented pace.

The AI boom is not happening by chance—it is the result of decades of technological progress, increasing computational power, vast amounts of data, and breakthroughs in machine learning and neural networks. But why now? Why is AI suddenly the most talked-about and rapidly growing industry in the world?

In this chapter, we will break down the key factors driving the AI boom, why this moment in history is critical, and what it means for businesses, entrepreneurs, and investors who want to capitalize on it.

The Convergence of Key Technologies: Why AI is Exploding Now

1. Increased Computing Power and Cloud Technology

AI requires immense computing power, and until recently, the hardware available could not efficiently support large-scale AI operations. However, advances in **Graphics Processing Units (GPUs), Tensor Processing Units (TPUs), and specialized AI chips** have made it possible to train and run sophisticated AI models at an affordable cost.

Cloud computing platforms like **Amazon Web Services (AWS), Google Cloud, and Microsoft Azure** now offer AI-as-a-service, allowing businesses and individuals to access cutting-edge AI tools without needing expensive hardware. This democratization of AI has made it accessible to startups, small businesses, and individuals, accelerating adoption and innovation.

2. The Rise of Big Data: Fueling AI Models

AI thrives on data. The more data an AI system is trained on, the smarter and more accurate it becomes. Over the past two decades, the world has produced an unprecedented amount of digital data—social media posts, search queries, transaction records, health data, GPS location tracking, and more.

Companies like Google, Meta, Amazon, and Tesla have built their AI models using massive datasets collected over years. **AI models like ChatGPT, Midjourney, and Stable Diffusion wouldn't be possible without the vast amounts of text, images, and structured data available today.**

The explosion of data has given AI the "fuel" it needs to grow at an exponential rate, making it more intelligent and capable with each iteration.

3. Breakthroughs in Machine Learning and Neural Networks

A major turning point in AI came with the development of **deep learning** and neural networks—complex algorithms designed to mimic the human brain's way of processing information. These models can recognize patterns, make predictions, and even "learn" from new data without direct programming.

In 2017, Google introduced the **Transformer model**, which dramatically improved AI's ability to process and generate human-like text. This technology powers modern AI systems like OpenAI's **GPT (Generative Pre-trained Transformer) models**, used in ChatGPT.

Additionally, advancements in **computer vision, reinforcement learning, and generative adversarial networks (GANs)** have enabled AI to create art, compose music, write essays, drive cars, and even diagnose diseases. These breakthroughs have made AI applications significantly more powerful and commercially viable.

4. Massive Investments in AI Development

Tech giants and governments worldwide are pouring billions of dollars into AI research and development. Companies like OpenAI, Google DeepMind, Meta, and Tesla are leading the charge, investing in AI to improve automation, advertising, self-driving cars, robotics, and virtual assistants.

In 2023 alone, **venture capital firms invested over $80 billion in AI startups**, and AI-driven companies saw an explosion in valuations. Microsoft's multi-billion-dollar investment in OpenAI, Google's Bard AI project, and Meta's AI research division all signal that AI is the future of business.

Governments are also recognizing the strategic importance of AI. **China and the U.S. are in an AI arms race**, both investing heavily in AI infrastructure, education, and national security applications. AI is now seen as a critical economic and military asset, further accelerating its development.

5. The Rise of AI in Everyday Applications

AI is no longer confined to research labs—it is becoming an essential part of everyday life. Consumers are using AI tools like:

- **ChatGPT** for writing, brainstorming, and coding
- **DALL·E and Midjourney** for AI-generated art
- **Siri and Google Assistant** for voice interactions
- **Tesla's Autopilot** for self-driving capabilities
- **AI-powered customer service chatbots** for automated support

Businesses are leveraging AI for **marketing automation, data analytics, fraud detection, and personalized customer experiences**, while freelancers are using AI for content creation, video editing, and coding assistance.

This widespread adoption is fueling further AI innovation and creating new markets, jobs, and revenue opportunities.

Why This Moment in History is Critical

1. AI is Replacing Traditional Jobs—But Creating New Ones

AI-driven automation is replacing jobs that involve repetitive tasks. Industries such as manufacturing, customer service, and even legal research are being transformed by AI-powered bots and software.

However, this shift is also **creating new high-paying opportunities** in AI development, prompt engineering, AI-assisted marketing, and AI integration consulting. Those who understand how to leverage AI—not just fear it—will be the ones who benefit the most.

2. The AI Market is Still in Its Early Stages

Although AI is making headlines, **we are still in the early adoption phase** of the AI revolution. Many businesses and industries are just beginning to integrate AI into their operations.

Historically, early adopters of transformative technology (such as the internet in the 1990s and social media in the 2000s) saw **massive financial gains**. Those who recognize AI's potential now and take action early can position themselves ahead of the competition.

3. AI Will Reshape Every Industry

AI is not limited to tech companies—it is transforming nearly every sector, including:

- **Healthcare:** AI-assisted diagnostics, robotic surgery, and personalized medicine
- **Finance:** AI-driven stock trading, fraud detection, and automated financial planning
- **E-commerce & Marketing:** AI-generated ads, chatbots, and personalized shopping experiences
- **Entertainment:** AI-generated movies, music, and interactive storytelling
- **Education:** AI-powered tutoring, adaptive learning platforms, and virtual teachers

This means that **no matter what industry you are in, AI will play a role in shaping its future**. Those who learn how to integrate AI into their careers or businesses will thrive.

Conclusion: The Time to Act is Now

The AI boom is happening at an unprecedented rate, and those who take advantage of it now will be in the best position to succeed. Whether you are looking to build a business, invest in AI companies, automate your work, or develop valuable AI skills, the opportunity is right in front of you.

AI is **not just a passing trend**—it is a technological revolution comparable to the rise of the internet. Ignoring it means being left behind, while embracing it can lead to financial success, career growth, and groundbreaking innovation.

In the next chapters, we will explore specific ways to **profit from AI**, from launching AI-powered businesses to investing in the right AI-driven opportunities. Now that you understand why AI is booming, it's time to position yourself to capitalize on the revolution.

The future belongs to those who recognize the power of AI—let's make sure you are one of them.

Chapter 2: The Best AI Startups to Watch in 2025

The AI revolution is accelerating, and startups are at the forefront of innovation. While tech giants like Google, Microsoft, and OpenAI continue to push AI forward, smaller AI-driven startups are pioneering groundbreaking applications in healthcare, finance, education, creative industries, and beyond.

If you want to invest in AI, work with AI-driven businesses, or launch your own AI-powered venture, understanding which startups are leading the charge is crucial. In this chapter, we'll explore the most promising AI startups of 2025, their impact on various industries, and how they are poised to disrupt the market.

The Criteria for Selecting the Top AI Startups

AI startups are emerging at an unprecedented rate, but not all will survive. The ones worth watching have:

- **Scalability** – Can the company expand rapidly with its AI solution?
- **Industry Disruption** – Is it solving a major problem or improving an industry significantly?
- **Funding & Investment** – Are venture capitalists and tech investors betting big on it?
- **Proven AI Models** – Does the startup have a working product with real-world applications?
- **Competitive Edge** – What makes it stand out from other AI companies?

Based on these criteria, let's dive into the **most exciting AI startups of 2025** and why they matter.

Top AI Startups to Watch in 2025
1. Anthropic – The Ethical AI Pioneer

- **What They Do:** Anthropic specializes in developing AI models with built-in safeguards to ensure responsible and ethical AI use. Their flagship AI, Claude, competes with ChatGPT but prioritizes safety and alignment with human values.
- **Why They Matter:** With growing concerns over AI ethics, bias, and misinformation, Anthropic's AI models are designed to be **less likely to produce harmful content** or be misused.
- **Industry Impact:** Conversational AI, enterprise AI solutions, and responsible AI deployment.
- **Funding & Growth:** Raised billions in funding from investors like Google and is rapidly scaling.

2. Mistral AI – The European AI Challenger

- **What They Do:** Mistral AI, based in France, is developing open-source AI models designed to rival those of OpenAI and Google DeepMind. Their focus is on **transparent, customizable, and modular AI models** that businesses can fine-tune.
- **Why They Matter:** Unlike closed AI systems, Mistral AI promotes **open-access AI**, allowing businesses to integrate AI without reliance on corporate-controlled models.
- **Industry Impact:** Enterprise AI, open-source AI solutions, and regulatory-compliant AI systems.
- **Funding & Growth:** Quickly securing funding and attracting European AI talent.

3. Runway ML – The Future of AI Video Creation

- **What They Do:** Runway ML is revolutionizing video production with **AI-powered video editing, special effects, and generative AI tools**. Their platform allows users to create Hollywood-level video content without extensive editing knowledge.
- **Why They Matter:** The AI-driven content creation market is booming, and Runway ML is leading the charge in **AI-generated films and synthetic media**.
- **Industry Impact:** Film, digital marketing, gaming, and social media.
- **Funding & Growth:** Secured major partnerships with creative agencies and studios.

4. Perplexity AI – The Google Disruptor

- **What They Do:** Perplexity AI is an **AI-powered search engine** that provides direct, conversational answers instead of traditional search result pages.
- **Why They Matter:** With **Google Search facing challenges from AI chatbots**, Perplexity AI offers an alternative that eliminates the need to click through multiple websites to find answers.
- **Industry Impact:** Search engines, content discovery, and knowledge management.
- **Funding & Growth:** Rapid adoption and a growing user base could make it a major Google competitor.

5. Hugging Face – The AI Developer's Best Friend

- **What They Do:** Hugging Face is a **hub for AI models, tools, and datasets**, allowing developers to build, train, and deploy AI applications easily.
- **Why They Matter:** AI development is becoming more accessible, and Hugging Face provides an essential **infrastructure for researchers and companies**.
- **Industry Impact:** Machine learning, AI model sharing, and enterprise AI applications.
- **Funding & Growth:** Backed by leading tech investors and expanding its AI marketplace.

6. Synthesia – The AI Video Spokesperson Company

- **What They Do:** Synthesia creates AI-generated avatars and virtual presenters for corporate training, marketing, and customer engagement.
- **Why They Matter:** Companies can now produce video content **without hiring actors, using studios, or extensive editing**.
- **Industry Impact:** Corporate training, advertising, and digital marketing.
- **Funding & Growth:** Partnering with major brands and expanding AI video solutions.

7. ElevenLabs – The Best AI Voice Generator

- **What They Do:** ElevenLabs specializes in **AI-generated voices** that are ultra-realistic, making them ideal for audiobooks, dubbing, and virtual assistants.
- **Why They Matter:** Their AI-generated voices are **nearly indistinguishable from real human speech**, making them invaluable for media, gaming, and automation.
- **Industry Impact:** Audiobooks, gaming, film, and AI-driven customer service.
- **Funding & Growth:** Strong adoption from content creators and media companies.

8. Character.AI – Personalized AI Chatbots

- **What They Do:** Character.AI allows users to create and chat with custom AI personalities, making AI interactions more engaging and personalized.
- **Why They Matter:** As AI becomes more integrated into daily life, Character.AI is redefining **personalized AI assistants and social AI interactions**.
- **Industry Impact:** Gaming, entertainment, and AI companionship.
- **Funding & Growth:** Gaining millions of active users and expanding its customization options.

9. OpenAI – Still the King of AI?

- **What They Do:** OpenAI is behind ChatGPT, DALL·E, and Codex, and continues to **set the benchmark for generative AI and automation**.
- **Why They Matter:** OpenAI's ongoing research and development **shape the AI industry** and influence competitors.
- **Industry Impact:** Conversational AI, creative AI, and enterprise AI applications.
- **Funding & Growth:** Massive investments from Microsoft and leading the AI ecosystem.

10. Humane – The AI Wearable Pioneer

- **What They Do:** Humane is developing **AI-powered wearable devices** that enhance human interaction with technology without relying on screens.
- **Why They Matter:** If successful, their AI-powered **wearable assistant could replace smartphones** as the dominant digital interface.
- **Industry Impact:** AI wearables, augmented reality, and consumer electronics.
- **Funding & Growth:** Backed by top-tier venture capitalists and former Apple executives.

How to Capitalize on These AI Startups

Now that you know the best AI startups to watch in 2025, here's how you can **profit from this AI boom**:

1. Invest in AI Startups Early

Many AI startups offer investment opportunities before they go public. **Look for AI-focused venture capital funds** or startup crowd-funding platforms that allow early-stage investments.

2. Use AI Tools to Scale Your Business

Startups like Hugging Face, Synthesia, and Runway ML provide AI tools that can automate tasks, enhance productivity, and create content. Leverage these AI platforms to grow your business faster.

3. Learn AI Skills in Demand

As AI startups grow, they need talent. **Prompt engineers, AI consultants, machine learning experts, and AI content creators** will be in high demand.

4. Start Your Own AI-Powered Business

AI is **lowering the barrier to entry** for startups. Whether it's AI-generated art, automated customer service, or AI-driven marketing, you can start your own AI-powered business with minimal costs.

Final Thoughts

The AI industry is expanding at lightning speed, and these startups are leading the way. Whether you invest in them, use their technology, or build your own AI-driven business, **2025 is the year to take action**.

Chapter 3: AI-Generated Content: New Ways to Make Money

The rise of artificial intelligence has unlocked new avenues for making money, and AI-generated content is at the forefront of this revolution. From writing and video production to art, music, and voiceovers, AI tools are enabling creators to produce high-quality content faster and at a lower cost than ever before. Whether you're an entrepreneur, freelancer, or business owner, understanding how to leverage AI-generated content can give you a significant advantage in today's digital economy.

This chapter explores the **best ways to make money with AI-generated content**, the **top AI tools** available, and a **step-by-step guide to launching your own AI-powered business**.

Why AI-Generated Content is a Game-Changer

AI-generated content is **disrupting traditional industries** by automating creative work that once required specialized skills. Businesses, marketers, and influencers are turning to AI to scale their operations, save time, and cut costs. Here's why AI-generated content is an opportunity you can't afford to ignore:

- **High Demand:** Businesses and brands need content at scale—AI makes it possible to meet this demand.
- **Low Barrier to Entry:** AI tools reduce the need for extensive skills, making it easier for beginners to enter creative fields.
- **Automation & Efficiency:** AI can generate content in minutes that would take humans hours or even days.
- **Scalability:** AI allows you to produce more content, increasing earning potential without additional effort.

Now, let's dive into **how you can make money with AI-generated content and launch a profitable AI-powered business**.

Ways to Make Money with AI-Generated Content

1. AI-Written Content & Blogging

AI writing tools can generate blog posts, ebooks, product descriptions, ad copy, and more. You can:

- Start a **niche blog** and use AI to write SEO-optimized posts, monetizing with ads or affiliate marketing.
- Offer **AI-generated writing services** on platforms like Fiverr, Upwork, or your own website.
- Create **AI-generated books** and self-publish them on Amazon Kindle Direct Publishing (KDP).

Top AI Writing Tools:

- **ChatGPT** (Content generation, blogs, and social media posts)
- **Jasper AI** (Marketing copy and long-form articles)
- **Copy.ai** (Ad copy, email campaigns, and sales pages)

2. AI-Generated Video Content

AI-powered video tools make it possible to create high-quality videos **without filming or hiring editors**. You can:

- Start a **YouTube channel** using AI-generated videos.
- Offer **AI video creation services** to businesses.
- Create **AI-generated explainer videos** for brands.

Top AI Video Tools:

- **Runway ML** (AI video editing and effects)
- **Synthesia** (AI avatars for business videos)
- **Pictory AI** (AI-powered video summarization and content re-purposing)

3. AI-Generated Art & Graphics

AI can generate **logos, illustrations, social media graphics, and NFTs**. You can:

- Sell **AI-generated art** on Etsy, Redbubble, or print-on-demand platforms.
- Offer **AI-generated logo design and branding services** to businesses.
- Create and sell **NFTs** based on AI-generated images.

Top AI Art Tools:

- **DALL·E 3** (AI-generated artwork and creative designs)
- **Midjourney** (High-quality AI art and illustrations)
- **Deep Dream Generator** (AI-based artistic transformations)

4. AI-Generated Music & Voiceovers

AI can generate background music, jingles, voiceovers, and narration. You can:

- Sell **AI-generated stock music** on sites like Pond5 and AudioJungle.
- Offer **voiceover services** for businesses, podcasters, and YouTubers.
- Create **audiobooks** with AI-generated voices and sell them on Audible.

Top AI Music & Voice Tools:

- **ElevenLabs** (Realistic AI voice generation)
- **AIVA** (AI-generated music composition)
- **Murph AI** (AI-powered voiceovers)

5. AI-Powered Course Creation

AI can help create entire online courses **faster than ever**. You can:

- Use AI to **generate course content** and sell courses on Udemy or Teachable.
- Automate **video lectures, quizzes, and scripts** using AI tools.
- Use AI chatbots to provide **student support and engagement**.

Top AI Course Creation Tools:

- **Descript** (AI-powered video editing and transcription)
- **ChatGPT** (Course content creation)
- **Synthesia** (AI avatar-driven video lectures)

How to Launch Your Own AI-Powered Business

Now that you know how to monetize AI-generated content, here's a **step-by-step guide to launching a profitable AI business**.

Step 1: Choose a Niche

Decide what type of AI-generated content you want to focus on. Consider:

- AI writing (blogs, ebooks, social media posts)
- AI video production (YouTube automation, explainer videos)
- AI art (NFTs, branding, graphic design)
- AI voiceovers and music (audiobooks, commercial jingles)

Pick a niche with **high demand and low competition** to maximize profitability.

Step 2: Select the Best AI Tools

Invest in AI tools that **match your niche**. For example:

- If creating AI-generated blogs → Use **ChatGPT** + **Jasper AI**
- If making AI videos → Use **Synthesia** + **Runway ML**
- If offering AI-generated voiceovers → Use **ElevenLabs** + **Murph AI**

Sign up for free trials and test different tools before committing to a paid plan.

Step 3: Create a Portfolio or Sample Work

Before landing clients or selling AI content, **create sample work** to showcase your AI-generated abilities. Examples:

- Publish **AI-generated blog posts** on a personal website.
- Create a **YouTube channel** with AI-generated videos.
- Upload **AI-generated digital art** to Etsy or Instagram.

A strong portfolio **attracts clients and builds credibility**.

Step 4: Choose a Monetization Model
There are several ways to make money with AI content:

- **Freelancing:** Offer AI-powered services on Fiverr, Upwork, or Toptal.
- **Selling Digital Products:** Sell AI-generated art, ebooks, or courses.
- **Subscriptions & Memberships:** Offer exclusive AI-generated content via Patreon or Substack.
- **Affiliate Marketing:** Promote AI tools and earn commissions.
- **Ads & Sponsorships:** Monetize AI-generated YouTube videos or blog content.

Choose a model that aligns with your **skills and business goals.**
Step 5: Market Your AI Business
To attract customers, use:

- **SEO & Blogging:** Write about AI-generated content on a blog.
- **Social Media:** Showcase AI work on Instagram, TikTok, LinkedIn, and Twitter.
- **YouTube & Video Marketing:** Create AI-generated videos to drive traffic.
- **Paid Ads & Email Marketing:** Use AI-generated ads to target potential clients.

Step 6: Automate & Scale Your AI Business
Once you start earning, **scale your business** by:

- Using AI to **automate repetitive tasks** (email responses, social media posts).
- Outsourcing additional work to **AI tools or freelancers**.
- Expanding into **new AI content types** (e.g., combining AI writing + AI video).

Final Thoughts: The Future of AI-Generated Content

AI-generated content is one of the **fastest-growing opportunities in the digital economy**. Those who take action **now** will be ahead of the curve, while those who hesitate may struggle to keep up.

Chapter 4: Investing in AI Stocks and Businesses

The artificial intelligence revolution is not just a technological shift—it's a financial opportunity. AI is reshaping industries, boosting company profits, and attracting massive investments from governments and corporations. If you want to build long-term wealth, investing in **AI stocks, startups, and blockchain projects** can position you at the forefront of this multi-trillion-dollar industry.

This chapter will guide you through **how to invest in AI, which stocks and startups to watch, and how blockchain intersects with AI to create even more investment opportunities**. Whether you're a beginner or an experienced investor, this roadmap will help you maximize your returns.

Why Invest in AI?

1. AI is Growing at an Exponential Rate

The global AI market was valued at **$150 billion in 2023** and is projected to exceed **$1.5 trillion by 2030**. Companies leveraging AI are **reducing costs, increasing efficiency, and generating new revenue streams**, making AI investments more lucrative than ever.

2. AI is the Future of Business

AI is **not a passing trend**—it's the backbone of future industries. Every major sector, including healthcare, finance, transportation, and retail, is integrating AI to stay competitive. **Investing in AI means investing in the future.**

3. AI Companies Have High Profit Margins

Unlike traditional businesses, AI-driven companies **scale easily and generate high profit margins**. AI-based SaaS (Software-as-a-Service) businesses, AI automation tools, and AI-powered customer service solutions allow companies to **make more money with fewer employees and lower operational costs**.

How to Invest in AI Stocks

Investing in AI stocks is one of the **easiest and safest ways** to gain exposure to the AI revolution. Here's a step-by-step guide to making smart AI stock investments:

Step 1: Understand the Types of AI Stocks

There are **three main categories** of AI stocks:

1. **AI Powerhouses (Tech Giants):**
    - These are large corporations that have heavily invested in AI development.
    - Examples: Microsoft, Google (Alphabet), Amazon, Nvidia, Meta.
2. **AI Infrastructure Companies:**
    - These companies **build the hardware and software** that power AI systems.
    - Examples: Nvidia (GPUs for AI), AMD, Broadcom, Snowflake, Palantir.
3. **AI-Driven Businesses:**
    - These are companies **using AI to transform their industries** (finance, healthcare, robotics, etc.).
    - Examples: Tesla (AI-powered autonomous driving), Intuitive Surgical (AI in medical robotics), C3.ai (AI enterprise solutions).

Step 2: Top AI Stocks to Watch in 2025

Here are **some of the best AI stocks to invest in** based on growth potential and market dominance:

1. Nvidia (NVDA) – The AI Hardware King

- **Why Invest?** Nvidia dominates the GPU market, which is essential for AI computing. Every major AI company relies on Nvidia's hardware.
- **Growth Potential:** Nvidia's AI-focused chips are in high demand, and the company is rapidly expanding into AI data centers and robotics.

2. Microsoft (MSFT) – The AI Software Leader

- **Why Invest?** Microsoft's multi-billion-dollar investment in OpenAI (the creators of ChatGPT) gives it a dominant position in AI-driven software.
- **Growth Potential:** AI is integrated into Microsoft's products, including Azure AI, Copilot, and Office 365, ensuring continued revenue growth.

3. Alphabet (GOOGL) – The AI Search and Cloud Giant

- **Why Invest?** Google is developing its own AI chatbot (Gemini), AI-powered search, and AI-driven advertising technology.
- **Growth Potential:** Google's AI ecosystem spans cloud computing, healthcare, and autonomous vehicles.

4. Amazon (AMZN) – AI in E-commerce and Cloud Computing

- **Why Invest?** Amazon is integrating AI into its retail platform and AWS cloud services.
- **Growth Potential:** AI-driven logistics, personalized shopping experiences, and Alexa voice technology fuel Amazon's AI expansion.

5. Tesla (TSLA) – AI and Autonomous Vehicles

- **Why Invest?** Tesla is at the forefront of AI-driven self-driving technology.
- **Growth Potential:** If Tesla perfects full autonomy, its valuation could skyrocket.

How to Invest in AI Startups

AI startups offer high-risk, high-reward opportunities. Unlike established companies, AI startups **have the potential to multiply investments tenfold or more**—but they also come with higher uncertainty.

Step 1: Where to Find AI Startups

To invest in AI startups before they go public, consider:

- **Angel Investing Platforms:** AngelList, SeedInvest, Republic.
- **Venture Capital Funds:** Invest indirectly by buying shares in AI-focused venture capital firms.
- **Crowdfunding Platforms:** Some AI startups allow small investors to participate through equity crowdfunding.

Step 2: AI Startups to Watch in 2025

Here are **some of the most promising AI startups** to consider investing in:

1. Anthropic – The Ethical AI Leader

- Building AI models focused on **safety and ethical AI alignment.**

2. Mistral AI – The Open-Source AI Challenger

- Competing with OpenAI by offering **modular, customizable AI solutions.**

3. Runway ML – AI for Video Creation

- Leading AI-generated **film and video content** technology.

4. Perplexity AI – The AI Search Engine Disruptor

- A **Google Search competitor** offering direct AI-generated answers.

5. ElevenLabs – AI Voice Generation

- Providing **hyper-realistic AI voices** for audiobooks, gaming, and media.

Investing in AI Blockchain Projects

Blockchain and AI are **merging to create decentralized AI models**, which could revolutionize data privacy, finance, and automation. Investing in AI-driven blockchain projects offers early access to **the next wave of AI disruption**.

Step 1: What Are AI Blockchain Projects?

AI blockchain projects integrate AI with **decentralized networks**, enabling:

- AI-powered **smart contracts and automation**.
- Decentralized AI models **that aren't controlled by big tech**.
- AI-generated **trading algorithms for crypto markets**.

Step 2: Top AI Blockchain Projects to Invest In

1. SingularityNET (AGIX) – Decentralized AI Services

- A marketplace where developers can **buy and sell AI services** using blockchain.

2. Fetch.AI (FET) – AI-Powered Automation

- AI-driven automation for **supply chains, finance, and digital transactions**.

3. Ocean Protocol (OCEAN) – AI Data Sharing

- Enables **secure, decentralized AI data sharing** for machine learning.

Investment Strategies for Long-Term AI Wealth

1. Diversify Your AI Investments

- Invest in **AI stocks for stability**.
- Invest in **AI startups for high-growth potential**.
- Invest in **AI blockchain projects for the future of AI decentralization**.

2. Buy and Hold for the Long Term

- AI stocks **will increase in value over time**, just like tech stocks did during the dot-com boom.
- Holding AI assets for 5-10 years could result in **massive returns**.

3. Stay Updated on AI Trends

- Follow AI news, earnings reports, and industry breakthroughs.
- Join AI investment groups, listen to AI tech podcasts, and track AI patents.

Final Thoughts: The AI Gold Rush is Just Beginning

AI is **the biggest technological revolution of our time**. Investing wisely in AI stocks, startups, and blockchain projects can **secure long-term wealth and financial freedom**.

Chapter 5: How to Use AI to Automate Income Streams

Artificial intelligence isn't just changing industries—it's revolutionizing **how people make money**. AI-powered automation is enabling entrepreneurs, freelancers, and investors to generate **passive income streams**, where money flows in with minimal ongoing effort. Whether you want to create digital products, automate a business, or build an AI-driven investment strategy, this chapter will show you **how to use AI to generate wealth while you sleep**.

If your goal is **financial independence**, learning to leverage AI automation is one of the most effective ways to achieve it **faster than traditional income models.**

Why AI-Powered Passive Income is the Future

1. AI Works 24/7

Unlike humans, AI doesn't take breaks. **Once set up, AI-driven businesses can run automatically**, allowing you to scale income without spending more time working.

2. Low Startup Costs & High Scalability

AI automation reduces costs **by replacing manual tasks**, enabling you to start a business or create digital assets **with minimal investment**. Once built, AI-driven income streams can grow exponentially.

3. Diversification of Income Sources

With AI, you can generate passive income from multiple sources at once—**AI-generated books, automated e-commerce, AI-powered stock trading, and more**.

Now, let's break down **how you can use AI to build passive income streams** in multiple industries.

How to Build Passive Income Streams with AI

1. AI-Generated Digital Products (Ebooks, Courses, & Printables)

How It Works:

- Use AI to create **ebooks, online courses, templates, or printables** and sell them on platforms like Amazon, Gumroad, Etsy, or Udemy.
- AI tools can generate content, design graphics, and even create voiceovers for online courses.

Step-by-Step Guide:

1. Use **ChatGPT** or **Jasper AI** to generate book content.
2. Use **Canva** or **Midjourney** to create book covers and templates.
3. Publish your digital product on Amazon KDP, Gumroad, or Etsy.
4. Automate marketing with AI-driven email sequences and social media ads.

Top AI Tools for Digital Products:

- **ChatGPT, Jasper AI** (AI writing)
- **Midjourney, Canva** (AI design & branding)
- **Synthesia, ElevenLabs** (AI video & voiceovers)

⍰ **Potential Earnings:** $500 – $10,000 per month **passively**.

2. AI-Powered Blogging & Content Websites
How It Works:

- AI can write **blog posts, SEO articles, and social media content** that generate organic traffic.
- Monetize through **display ads, affiliate marketing, and sponsored posts**.

Step-by-Step Guide:

1. Use **ChatGPT or SurferSEO** to generate high-ranking blog content.
2. Automate blog scheduling with **WordPress AI plugins**.
3. Use **AI chatbots** for customer interaction and lead generation.
4. Monetize with **Google AdSense, affiliate links, and digital product sales**.

Top AI Tools for Blogging:

- **SurferSEO, RankMath** (SEO optimization)
- **Copy.ai, Jasper AI** (AI-powered content writing)
- **WordPress AI Plugins** (Content scheduling, AI chatbots)

⟐ **Potential Earnings:** $1,000 – $30,000 per month **passively**.

3. AI-Automated YouTube Channels

How It Works:

- AI-generated videos can be **fully automated**, requiring no filming or editing skills.
- Monetize through **YouTube ads, sponsorships, and affiliate marketing**.

Step-by-Step Guide:

1. Use **ChatGPT** to generate video scripts.
2. Use **Synthesia or Runway ML** to create AI-generated videos.
3. Automate video editing with **Descript**.
4. Post AI-generated YouTube Shorts and long-form videos.
5. Monetize through **Google AdSense, sponsorships, and affiliate links**.

Top AI Tools for YouTube Automation:

- **Synthesia, Runway ML** (AI video creation)
- **ElevenLabs, Murph AI** (AI voiceovers)
- **Descript, Pictory** (AI video editing)

◈ **Potential Earnings:** $1,000 – $50,000 per month **passively**.

4. AI-Driven Affiliate Marketing
How It Works:

- AI can automate **content creation, email marketing, and sales funnels**, allowing you to **promote products and earn commissions on autopilot.**

Step-by-Step Guide:

1. Use AI to build a niche website with **blog posts and reviews.**
2. Automate traffic generation with AI-powered social media bots.
3. Use AI email automation tools to send promotional emails.
4. Monetize through **Amazon Associates, ClickBank, and ShareASale.**

Top AI Tools for Affiliate Marketing:

- **ChatGPT, Jasper AI** (AI-generated affiliate articles)
- **ConvertKit, Mailchimp AI** (AI-powered email automation)
- **Outgrow AI** (AI-powered interactive quizzes for lead generation)

◈ **Potential Earnings:** $500 – $25,000 per month **passively.**

5. AI-Driven Automated E-Commerce (Dropshipping & Print-on-Demand)
How It Works:

- AI automates **product research, store setup, and marketing** for e-commerce businesses.
- Monetize through **dropshipping, print-on-demand, and AI-generated product branding**.

Step-by-Step Guide:

1. Use **AI product research tools** to find trending items.
2. Build an online store using **Shopify AI or WooCommerce**.
3. Use AI-generated designs for **print-on-demand products**.
4. Automate marketing with **AI ad optimization tools**.

Top AI Tools for E-Commerce:

- **Sell The Trend, Niche Scraper** (AI-driven product research)
- **Shopify AI, Printify, Redbubble** (AI-powered store automation)
- **AdCreative.ai, ChatGPT** (AI-powered marketing and customer support)

◈ **Potential Earnings:** $2,000 – $50,000 per month **passively**.

6. AI-Powered Stock Trading & Crypto Investing
How It Works:

- AI-powered algorithms can **automate stock and crypto trading** for passive income.

Step-by-Step Guide:

1. Use **AI trading bots** to analyze stock and crypto market trends.
2. Automate buying and selling using **AI-powered trading platforms**.
3. Monitor performance with **AI analytics tools**.

Top AI Tools for Automated Investing:

- **Trade Ideas, Tickeron** (AI-powered stock trading bots)
- **3Commas, Cryptohopper** (AI crypto trading bots)
- **Zignaly, Numerai** (AI hedge fund investing)

◈ **Potential Earnings:** Varies based on market conditions.

Final Thoughts: AI-Powered Passive Income Can Change Your Life

AI automation allows **anyone to build multiple passive income streams** with minimal effort. Whether you choose **blogging, YouTube automation, e-commerce, or AI investing, the key is to start now before markets get saturated.**

Chapter 6: The Rise of AI Art, Music, and Creativity

Artificial Intelligence is revolutionizing the creative industries, blurring the lines between human creativity and machine-generated content. AI-generated art, music, and writing have evolved from experimental projects into powerful tools that freelancers, entrepreneurs, and artists can use to **make money online, build businesses, and automate creative work.**

In this chapter, we'll explore how AI is transforming **art, music, and digital creativity**, and how freelancers and remote workers can **capitalize on AI tools to build profitable careers**. Whether you're an artist, musician, writer, or content creator, AI is unlocking new revenue streams that were never possible before.

How AI is Transforming Art, Music, and Creativity

For centuries, artistic and musical expression have been uniquely human endeavors. However, with advances in **machine learning, neural networks, and generative AI**, technology can now **create art, compose music, and even mimic human creativity** with astonishing precision.

1. AI-Generated Art & Design

AI-powered art tools can create **stunning digital artwork, illustrations, and branding materials** in seconds. Artists and designers are using AI to:

- Generate **logos, posters, and digital paintings**.
- Create **NFT collections and digital assets**.
- Sell AI-generated art on platforms like **Etsy, Redbubble, and print-on-demand services**.

2. AI-Generated Music & Audio

AI music generators can **compose original music, background scores, and jingles** for movies, video games, and content creators. AI-generated voiceovers and soundtracks are being used in:

- **Podcasting, audiobooks, and narration.**
- **Music production and commercial jingles.**
- **YouTube videos and AI-generated movies.**

3. AI-Generated Writing & Content Creation

AI is also transforming the **publishing, content writing, and copywriting industries.** AI tools can now generate:

- **Full-length books, blog posts, and marketing copy.**
- **AI-driven storytelling and screenplays.**
- **Social media posts, ad copy, and email marketing campaigns.**

The demand for AI-generated content is skyrocketing, creating **lucrative opportunities for freelancers and online business owners.**

How AI is Revolutionizing Freelancing and Remote Work

AI is **leveling the playing field** for freelancers by automating tedious tasks, **increasing productivity, and creating new job opportunities**. Whether you want to **start an online business, work remotely, or generate passive income**, AI tools can help you scale your work and increase your earnings.

1. AI-Powered Freelancing Careers

If you're looking for **AI-driven freelance jobs**, here are the **most profitable AI-powered careers**:

A. AI-Generated Art & Graphic Design

◈ **How to Make Money:**

- Sell **AI-generated logos and branding kits** on Fiverr and Upwork.
- Sell **AI art prints, stock images, and posters** on Etsy, Printify, or Redbubble.
- Offer **AI-generated NFT design services**.

◈ **Best AI Tools:**

- **Midjourney** (AI-generated artwork)
- **DALL·E 3** (Text-to-image AI generator)
- **Runway ML** (AI-based design and animation)

B. AI-Powered Content Writing & Blogging

◈ **How to Make Money:**

- Start a blog using AI-generated SEO content and monetize with ads and affiliate marketing.
- Offer **AI-powered writing services** (ebooks, copywriting, social media posts).
- Sell **AI-generated newsletters or niche content subscriptions**.

◈ **Best AI Tools:**

- **ChatGPT** (Content creation & blog writing)
- **Jasper AI** (Marketing and ad copy)
- **Copy.ai** (Automated sales and email writing)

C. AI Voiceovers & Podcasting

◈ **How to Make Money:**

- Sell **AI-generated voiceover services** for YouTube creators and businesses.
- Create and monetize an **AI-narrated podcast**.
- Offer **AI audiobook narration services** on ACX (Audible's publishing platform).

◈ **Best AI Tools:**

- **ElevenLabs** (AI-generated voiceovers)
- **Murph AI** (Realistic AI narration)
- **Descript** (AI-powered audio editing)

D. AI Video Editing & YouTube Automation

⟐ **How to Make Money:**

- Start an **AI-automated YouTube channel** (without filming anything).
- Offer **AI-powered video editing services**.
- Sell **AI-generated explainer videos** to businesses.

⟐ **Best AI Tools:**

- **Synthesia** (AI-generated talking avatars)
- **Pictory** (AI video creation from text)
- **Runway ML** (AI video editing and animation)

How to Use AI to Build a Profitable Freelancing Business

Now that you know **which AI-powered jobs are in demand**, here's how you can start your **AI-driven freelancing business** step by step.

Step 1: Choose an AI Niche

Pick a service that has **high demand and low competition**. Examples:

◈ AI-generated logos and branding
◈ AI blog writing and SEO content
◈ AI voiceover services for YouTube
◈ AI video animation for businesses

Step 2: Create a Portfolio Using AI Tools

Before getting clients, create **sample work** showcasing your AI-powered skills.

- **For AI Art** → Create a collection of 10+ AI-generated designs.
- **For AI Writing** → Publish 5+ AI-generated articles on a personal blog.
- **For AI Video Editing** → Upload 2-3 AI-generated video samples to YouTube.

Step 3: List Your Services on Freelance Platforms

Join top freelancing sites to find clients:

◈ **Fiverr** (AI logo design, AI video editing, AI blog writing)
◈ **Upwork** (AI content creation, AI social media management)
◈ **PeoplePerHour** (AI-powered business services)

Step 4: Automate Your Work for Maximum Income

Once you start getting clients, **use AI automation to scale your business**:

- **Chatbots for customer service** (ChatGPT-powered responses).
- **AI scheduling tools** (Zapier & Calendly) to automate orders.
- **AI invoicing tools** (FreshBooks & QuickBooks) for effortless payments.

Step 5: Scale Your AI Business to Passive Income

To go from **freelancer to business owner**, create **digital assets** that generate **passive income**:

◈ Sell **AI art bundles** as stock images.

◈ Create **AI-generated eBooks** and sell them on Amazon.

◈ Launch a **YouTube channel with AI-generated content**.

◈ **Earning Potential:** $5,000 – $100,000 per month **passively**.

Final Thoughts: The AI Creative Boom is Just Beginning

The demand for **AI-generated content is skyrocketing**, and **freelancers who adopt AI will earn more while working less**. Whether you choose **AI-powered art, music, writing, or video creation**, now is the **best time to start making money online with AI tools**.

Chapter 7: Ethical Considerations in AI Money-Making

Artificial Intelligence has opened new doors for entrepreneurship, automation, and wealth creation, but with these opportunities come ethical challenges. As AI continues to reshape the business landscape, **understanding the ethical implications of AI-driven money-making is crucial.**

In this chapter, we'll explore:

- The **ethical concerns** surrounding AI in business and content creation.
- The **responsible use of AI** in freelancing, investing, and entrepreneurship.
- **How to launch a fully automated AI-powered business** while maintaining ethical integrity.

For entrepreneurs looking to **scale their businesses with AI**, it's important to **balance profitability with responsible AI usage**.

The Ethical Challenges of AI in Business

As AI becomes a key player in generating wealth, **certain ethical dilemmas arise**. Entrepreneurs and freelancers must consider:

1. AI and Job Displacement

AI automation is **replacing traditional jobs** in customer service, content creation, graphic design, and even software development. The question is:

- **How can AI entrepreneurs profit without harming workers?**
- **How can AI complement human jobs rather than eliminate them?**

⯑ **Ethical Solution:** AI should be used to **enhance productivity and support workers** rather than replace them entirely. Businesses should **train workers in AI skills** to transition them into higher-value roles.

2. AI-Generated Content and Plagiarism

AI can generate **written content, images, and videos**, but in some cases, **it pulls from copyrighted material**. Entrepreneurs need to ensure that their **AI-generated work is original and not infringing on someone else's intellectual property**.

⯑ **Ethical Solution:**

- Use AI tools that **generate content from scratch** instead of reusing existing work.
- Always **credit AI-generated content** when applicable (e.g., "Created using AI").
- Avoid using AI to replicate **a specific artist's or author's style** without permission.

3. AI Deepfakes and Misinformation

AI is now capable of **creating hyper-realistic deepfake videos, cloned voices, and fabricated news articles**. If misused, AI can spread **misinformation, fraud, and identity theft**.

◈ **Ethical Solution:**

- Never use AI to **deceive or manipulate**.
- Clearly disclose AI-generated media in advertisements and branding.
- Use AI for **educational, creative, or entertainment purposes** rather than deception.

4. Bias in AI Algorithms

AI models **learn from data**, and if the data contains biases, **AI-generated results may be unfair** (e.g., racial, gender, or economic bias in hiring tools, loan approvals, and recommendation engines).

◈ **Ethical Solution:**

- Use **AI models trained on diverse datasets**.
- Regularly audit AI decision-making processes to **reduce bias**.
- Choose **transparent AI tools** that allow customization and oversight.

How to Launch an AI-Powered Business That Runs on Autopilot

Now that we've covered **the ethical considerations of AI-driven money-making**, let's dive into how you can **build a fully automated AI-powered business that generates passive income** while staying ethical and sustainable.

Step 1: Choose a Profitable AI Business Model

A successful AI-powered business should be:

⯑ **Scalable** (able to grow without constant input)

⯑ **Automated** (requires minimal manual work)

⯑ **Ethical** (does not exploit, deceive, or infringe on rights)

AI Business Ideas:

- **AI-Powered Content Creation** → Automated blogs, video editing, and ebooks.
- **AI Consulting Services** → Teaching businesses how to integrate AI.
- **AI Chatbot Business** → Automating customer support for companies.
- **AI-Generated Digital Products** → Selling AI-created art, courses, and templates.
- **AI-Powered E-Commerce** → Automated dropshipping or print-on-demand.

⯑ **Top AI Tools for Automation:**

- **Jasper AI & ChatGPT** → Automated content writing.
- **Midjourney & DALL·E** → AI-generated digital art.
- **Synthesia & Runway ML** → AI-generated videos.
- **ElevenLabs & Murph AI** → AI voiceovers.

Step 2: Set Up AI for Maximum Automation

A **fully automated AI business** should have minimal manual intervention. Here's how to set it up:

A. Automate Content Creation

- Use **ChatGPT** to generate blog posts and SEO content.
- Use **DALL·E or Midjourney** for digital artwork and product designs.
- Use **Pictory AI** to turn text into AI-generated videos.

B. Automate Customer Interactions

- Set up an **AI chatbot** (e.g., ManyChat, ChatGPT API) to **handle customer inquiries**.
- Use **AI-powered email marketing** (e.g., ConvertKit AI, Mailchimp) to nurture leads.

C. Automate Order Fulfillment & Sales

- Use **Shopify AI or Printify AI** for **automated e-commerce**.
- Use **AI-powered ad targeting** (e.g., AdCreative.ai) to **run paid marketing campaigns** without manual oversight.

◈ **Once these systems are in place, the business runs on autopilot!**

Step 3: Monetize Your AI-Powered Business

Once your AI business is set up, you need to **monetize it effectively**. Here's how:

⟐ **Selling AI-Generated Digital Products**

- Create and sell **AI-generated ebooks** on Amazon KDP.
- Sell **AI-generated art and printables** on Etsy.
- Offer **AI-designed website templates** on Gumroad.

⟐ **Affiliate Marketing & Subscription Services**

- Promote **AI tools and services** and earn commissions (Jasper AI, Canva AI, etc.).
- Set up a **paid membership site** offering exclusive AI-generated content.

⟐ **AI-Powered E-Commerce & Dropshipping**

- Automate **AI-designed print-on-demand merchandise**.
- Sell **AI-generated custom logos and branding kits**.

⟐ **Potential Earnings:** $5,000 – $100,000+ per month **passively**.

Step 4: Scale Your AI Business Ethically

⟐ **To grow your AI business, ensure it remains ethical and responsible:**

⟐ **Disclose AI-generated content** to customers.
⟐ **Offer value-based AI products** (not spammy or low-quality).
⟐ **Comply with copyright laws** when using AI-generated content.
⟐ **Adapt to AI regulations** to future-proof your business.

Final Thoughts: AI Ethics and Financial Freedom Can Coexist

The AI revolution presents **unprecedented opportunities to build wealth**, but entrepreneurs must **use AI responsibly**.

By **launching an AI-powered business that runs on autopilot**, you can:

⟐ Generate **passive income** with minimal work.
⟐ Scale your business **ethically and sustainably**.
⟐ Future-proof your income **in the AI-driven economy**.

Chapter 8: AI in Marketing and E-Commerce

Artificial Intelligence (AI) is **redefining the future of marketing and e-commerce**, allowing businesses to reach the right customers with hyper-personalized strategies and automate sales like never before. Companies that integrate AI into their marketing and e-commerce strategies are seeing **higher conversion rates, increased revenue, and reduced operational costs**.

At the same time, **AI is transforming the job market**, creating new opportunities while automating many traditional roles. To stay relevant and profitable in the AI-driven economy, entrepreneurs, freelancers, and employees must **adapt to AI-powered tools and business models**.

In this chapter, we will explore:

- How **AI is revolutionizing digital marketing** and online sales.
- How to **use AI to build a profitable e-commerce business**.
- How AI is **changing the future of work** and what you need to do to **stay ahead of automation**.

How AI is Revolutionizing Digital Marketing

AI is **eliminating guesswork** from marketing by analyzing vast amounts of data to predict consumer behavior, optimize ad campaigns, and personalize content at scale.

1. AI-Powered Content Marketing

AI can **write blog posts, generate social media content, and create ad copy**—allowing businesses to scale content marketing without hiring large teams.

◈ **How to Use AI for Content Marketing:**

- Use **ChatGPT** or **Jasper AI** to generate SEO-friendly blog posts and articles.
- Use **Copy.ai** or **Writesonic** for ad copy, social media captions, and email campaigns.
- Use **SurferSEO** to optimize AI-generated content for search engines.

◈ **How to Profit from AI Content Marketing:**

- Offer **AI-powered blog writing services** to businesses.
- Start a **niche blog** and monetize it with affiliate marketing.
- Sell **AI-generated social media content packages** on Fiverr or Upwork.

2. AI-Driven Social Media Marketing

AI **automates social media management, content scheduling, and audience engagement**, allowing businesses to grow their presence **without spending hours on manual posting**.

◈ **How to Use AI for Social Media Marketing:**

- Use **Predis.ai** or **Lately AI** to generate and schedule social media posts.
- Use **Canva AI** to create automated social media graphics.
- Use **Hootsuite AI** to track performance and engagement analytics.

◈ **How to Profit from AI Social Media Marketing:**

- Offer **AI-powered social media management** services to small businesses.
- Grow a **niche Instagram or TikTok account** and monetize through sponsorships.
- Automate and sell **AI-generated social media templates** on Etsy or Gumroad.

3. AI-Powered Paid Advertising & Lead Generation

AI can optimize ad campaigns **faster and more accurately than human marketers**, increasing ROI on paid ads.

◈ **How to Use AI for Paid Ads & Lead Generation:**

- Use **AdCreative.ai** to generate high-converting Facebook and Google ads.
- Use **Persado AI** to craft persuasive ad copy and A/B test variations.
- Use **Chatbots (ManyChat, Drift AI)** to **automate lead capture and sales conversations.**

◈ **How to Profit from AI in Paid Advertising:**

- Start a **Facebook & Google AI Ads Agency** and help businesses scale ads.
- Offer **AI chatbot automation** services for lead generation.
- Use AI to optimize **your own affiliate marketing and dropshipping ads**.

How AI is Transforming E-Commerce

AI is revolutionizing online shopping, making it easier for businesses to **predict consumer behavior, personalize product recommendations, and automate order fulfillment.**

1. AI-Driven Product Research & Market Trends

AI tools can **analyze millions of online searches** to identify trending products before they go viral.

◈ **How to Use AI for Product Research:**

- Use **Sell The Trend** or **Niche Scraper** to find **winning products** for dropshipping.
- Use **Google Trends AI** to identify **rising product categories.**
- Use **Jungle Scout AI** to analyze **Amazon sales trends.**

◈ **How to Profit from AI Product Research:**

- Start an **AI-optimized dropshipping store.**
- Sell AI-researched **niche print-on-demand products.**
- Offer **AI-driven product research services** to e-commerce sellers.

2. AI-Powered Personalization & Customer Experience

AI **enhances online shopping experiences by personalizing recommendations and automating customer interactions.**

◈ **How to Use AI for Personalization:**

- Use **Dynamic Yield AI** to personalize e-commerce store layouts.
- Use **Klaviyo AI** to create **AI-driven email marketing sequences.**
- Use **Tidio AI Chatbots** to automate **customer service responses.**

◈ **How to Profit from AI-Powered E-Commerce:**

- Start an **AI-driven print-on-demand store.**
- Sell **personalized AI-generated product recommendations.**
- Offer **AI chatbot integration services** to Shopify store owners.

3. AI-Powered Dropshipping & Print-on-Demand

AI **fully automates the process** of selling products without holding inventory.

◈ **How to Use AI for Automated E-Commerce:**

- Use **Shopify AI & Oberlo AI** for **automated dropshipping fulfillment**.
- Use **Printify AI & Redbubble** for **on-demand AI-generated designs**.
- Use **AI pricing tools** (Dynamic Pricing AI) to optimize profit margins.

◈ **How to Profit from AI E-Commerce:**

- Create **AI-generated clothing and print-on-demand designs**.
- Launch a **fully automated Shopify dropshipping store**.
- Offer **AI e-commerce automation services** to other sellers.

The Future of Work in the AI Economy

As AI takes over **repetitive marketing and e-commerce tasks**, the **job market is changing.**

How to Stay Relevant and Profitable in the AI-Driven Job Market

◈ **1. Learn AI Skills (Even If You're Not a Developer)**

- Understand **AI-driven marketing tools** like ChatGPT, AdCreative, and Jasper.
- Learn how to integrate **AI chatbots and automation** into businesses.
- Stay updated on **AI trends in social media and e-commerce**.

◈ **2. Shift to High-Value, AI-Augmented Roles**

Jobs that involve **human creativity, strategy, and emotional intelligence** will remain in demand.

- AI **can't replace brand storytelling, marketing strategy, and emotional connections**.
- Entrepreneurs who **use AI to scale their businesses** (instead of fearing it) will thrive.

◈ **3. Build AI-Powered Passive Income Streams**

- Start an **AI-automated marketing agency**.
- Sell **AI-generated digital products**.
- Build a **passive-income AI e-commerce business**.

◈ **Key Takeaway:** Those who learn **how to use AI to create value** will have **endless job opportunities and income streams**.

Final Thoughts: AI is the Future of Marketing & E-Commerce

The AI-driven economy is already here. Businesses that **integrate AI into their marketing and e-commerce strategies** will dominate the digital landscape.

◈ **Key Business Takeaways:**

◈ AI can **automate marketing, content creation, and ad campaigns.**

◈ AI can **personalize e-commerce experiences and optimize sales.**

◈ AI-powered **dropshipping and print-on-demand stores** can run on autopilot.

◈ **Key Career Takeaways:**

◈ Learn **AI-powered marketing & automation tools.**

◈ Focus on **high-value creative & strategic roles AI can't replace.**

◈ Build **AI-driven passive income streams to future-proof your finances.**

Chapter 9: Freelancing with AI: Tools That Increase Profits

The rise of **Artificial Intelligence (AI) is transforming freelancing**, enabling professionals to automate tasks, increase productivity, and scale their businesses like never before. Freelancers who leverage AI tools can **work faster, charge higher rates, and build multiple income streams** while reducing manual labor.

At the same time, AI is reshaping the job market, and **understanding where AI is headed** is crucial for freelancers who want to **stay relevant and profitable in an AI-driven world**.

In this chapter, we will explore:

◈ The **top AI tools** that help freelancers **increase profits and automate work**.

◈ The **best AI-powered freelancing careers** and **how to make money with them**.

◈ **The future of AI and how to position yourself for long-term success.**

Why AI is the Ultimate Profit Booster for Freelancers

1. AI Automates Repetitive Tasks

Freelancers no longer have to spend **hours writing, editing, designing, or managing emails**—AI can **automate** these processes, allowing them to **focus on high-value work** and **take on more clients**.

2. AI Enables High-Quality Work with Less Effort

AI-powered tools **enhance writing, design, video editing, and research**, making it possible to **deliver professional-level work faster and at scale**.

3. AI Increases Earnings Through Automation

By using AI to create **multiple passive income streams**, freelancers can **diversify their revenue and make money 24/7** without constantly working.

Best AI Tools for Freelancers to Increase Profits

1. AI Writing & Content Generation

◈ **Freelance Jobs You Can Do with AI Writing Tools:**

- Blog writing, copywriting, and SEO articles.
- Ad copy and sales page creation.
- Email marketing and newsletters.

◈ **Best AI Writing Tools:**

- **ChatGPT** → Generates blog posts, ad copy, and research summaries.
- **Jasper AI** → AI-powered content creation for businesses.
- **Copy.ai** → Writes social media posts, emails, and sales copy.

◈ **How to Make Money:**

- Offer **AI-powered writing services** on Fiverr or Upwork.
- Create and sell **AI-generated blog posts** to companies.
- Use AI to **write and self-publish books** on Amazon KDP.

◈ **Earning Potential:** $3,000 – $15,000 per month.

2. AI Graphic Design & Digital Art

◈ **Freelance Jobs You Can Do with AI Design Tools:**

- Logo design and branding.
- Social media graphics and marketing materials.
- AI-generated art and print-on-demand products.

◈ **Best AI Graphic Design Tools:**

- **Midjourney** → Creates AI-generated artwork and logos.
- **DALL·E 3** → Generates unique AI-based illustrations.
- **Canva AI** → Automates social media design and branding.

◈ **How to Make Money:**

- Sell **AI-generated art prints** on Etsy or Redbubble.
- Offer **logo design services** using AI tools.
- Start a **print-on-demand business** with AI-generated designs.

◈ **Earning Potential:** $2,000 – $12,000 per month.

3. AI Video Editing & YouTube Automation

◈ **Freelance Jobs You Can Do with AI Video Tools:**

- YouTube automation and AI video creation.
- AI-enhanced video editing for businesses.
- AI-generated explainer videos and ads.

◈ **Best AI Video Editing Tools:**

- **Runway ML** → AI-powered video effects and editing.
- **Synthesia** → AI avatars and voiceovers for video content.
- **Pictory** → AI-generated video summaries from text.

◈ **How to Make Money:**

- Start a **fully automated YouTube channel** with AI-generated content.
- Offer **AI-powered video editing services** to content creators.
- Create and sell **AI-generated explainer videos** to businesses.

◈ **Earning Potential:** $5,000 – $50,000 per month.

4. AI Voiceovers & Podcasting

◈ Freelance Jobs You Can Do with AI Voice Tools:

- AI-generated audiobook narration.
- AI voiceovers for YouTube, ads, and corporate videos.
- AI-generated podcasting and storytelling.

◈ Best AI Voiceover Tools:

- **ElevenLabs** → AI-generated voices for narration.
- **Murph AI** → Human-like AI voiceovers for businesses.
- **Descript** → AI-based audio and podcast editing.

◈ How to Make Money:

- Sell **AI-generated voiceovers** to businesses.
- Launch an **AI-powered podcast and monetize it**.
- Offer **AI audiobook narration** services.

◈ Earning Potential: $2,500 – $15,000 per month.

How to Build a Fully AI-Powered Freelancing Business

Step 1: Choose an AI-Optimized Niche

Pick a freelance service where AI **enhances your efficiency and earning potential**:

◈ AI blog writing & SEO content creation.
◈ AI-generated video editing & YouTube automation.
◈ AI voiceovers & podcasting services.

Step 2: Set Up AI Automation

Use AI to **automate content creation, scheduling, and client communication**.

- Use **Chatbots (ManyChat, Drift AI)** to handle **client inquiries automatically**.
- Use **Zapier AI** to connect apps and **automate workflows**.
- Use **AI scheduling tools (Calendly AI)** to **manage bookings without manual effort**.

Step 3: Market Your AI Services & Scale

- Create an **AI-powered freelance website** to showcase your work.
- Promote services through **AI-optimized social media marketing.**
- Sell AI-generated **digital products, templates, or courses** for passive income.

◈ **Earning Potential:** $10,000 – $100,000+ per month when scaled.

The Future of AI: Where It's Heading Next

AI is **rapidly evolving**, and freelancers need to **stay ahead of trends** to remain profitable.

◈ **1. AI Will Continue to Automate Low-Skill Jobs**

- Routine tasks in writing, design, and marketing will be **fully automated.**
- Freelancers must **shift to AI-enhanced roles** that require creativity and strategic thinking.

◈ **2. AI-Powered Virtual Assistants Will Dominate the Job Market**

- AI will handle **email communication, social media, and project management.**
- Entrepreneurs and freelancers who **leverage AI automation** will **earn more while working less.**

◈ **3. The Rise of AI-Enhanced Gig Work**

- Freelancing will **move from manual work to AI-augmented consulting.**
- Businesses will pay **premium rates for AI-powered expertise** rather than raw labor.

◈ **4. AI-Powered Businesses Will Scale Faster**

- The most successful freelancers will **transition into AI-powered agencies.**
- **Those who learn to use AI now will have a major advantage** in the evolving job market.

Final Thoughts: Positioning Yourself for Long-Term Success in the AI Economy

To **stay ahead in the AI-driven world**, freelancers must:

◈ **Master AI tools** and integrate them into their work.

◈ **Move from low-skill to AI-augmented consulting and business automation.**

◈ **Build multiple AI-driven income streams for financial security**.

◈ **Adopt AI as a partner rather than fearing it as a competitor.**

◈ **Freelancers who embrace AI today will dominate the future of work.**

Chapter 10: How AI Will Shape Future Job Markets and How to Stay Ahead

Artificial Intelligence (AI) is transforming the global workforce, redefining industries, and automating business processes at an unprecedented rate. The AI revolution is creating **new job opportunities while eliminating traditional roles**, and those who fail to adapt may find themselves struggling to compete.

At the same time, **AI is enabling entrepreneurs to build multi-million-dollar businesses with minimal overhead**, allowing companies to scale faster, automate operations, and maximize profits.

In this **final chapter**, we will explore:

⟐ How **AI is reshaping the job market** and which industries will be most affected.

⟐ **The skills you need to stay ahead** and future-proof your career.

⟐ How **entrepreneurs can use AI to build scalable, high-revenue businesses** with minimal expenses.

How AI is Reshaping the Global Job Market

The job market is undergoing **a fundamental transformation**, driven by AI's ability to **automate repetitive tasks, optimize decision-making, and enhance productivity**.

1. AI Will Replace Many Low-Skill Jobs

◈ Jobs at High Risk of Automation:

- **Data Entry Clerks & Administrative Assistants** → AI can process and organize data faster.
- **Customer Service Representatives** → AI chatbots handle millions of inquiries 24/7.
- **Retail Cashiers & Warehouse Workers** → AI-powered self-checkouts and robots are replacing human workers.

◈ Future Outlook:

Routine and repetitive tasks will be automated, but humans will still be needed for **problem-solving, creativity, and emotional intelligence**.

2. AI Will Create New High-Paying Careers
◈ **Fastest-Growing AI-Related Careers:**

- **AI Consultants** → Help businesses integrate AI into their workflows.
- **Prompt Engineers** → Specialize in training and fine-tuning AI-generated content.
- **AI Cybersecurity Experts** → Prevent AI-related fraud and hacking threats.
- **AI-Powered Digital Marketing Strategists** → Optimize AI-driven ad campaigns.

◈ **Future Outlook:**
Workers who **adapt to AI-enhanced roles** will have **higher salaries and more job security**.
3. AI Will Reshape Traditional Industries
◈ **Industries AI Will Disrupt the Most:**

- **Healthcare** → AI-powered diagnostics, robotic surgery, and patient monitoring.
- **Finance** → AI-driven stock trading, fraud detection, and personalized financial advice.
- **Legal** → AI document review, contract analysis, and case predictions.
- **Manufacturing** → AI-driven quality control, robotics, and predictive maintenance.

◈ **Future Outlook:**
AI **won't eliminate jobs—it will change them. Workers who embrace AI tools will outperform those who resist them.**

How to Stay Ahead in the AI Job Market

To **future-proof your career**, you need to **develop AI-related skills** and **position yourself as a valuable asset** in an AI-driven world.

1. Master AI Tools & Automation

◈ Learn **AI-powered productivity tools**:

- **ChatGPT & Jasper AI** (Writing & communication automation).
- **Midjourney & Canva AI** (Graphic design & content creation).
- **Runway ML & Synthesia** (AI-generated video & multimedia).
- **ElevenLabs & Murph AI** (AI voice generation & audio editing).

◈ **Action Plan:**

Take **online AI courses**, experiment with AI tools, and apply them to your work immediately.

2. Shift to AI-Augmented Careers

◈ **Transition into roles that integrate AI:**

- **AI Marketing Specialists** → Optimize AI-driven ad campaigns.
- **AI-Powered Customer Experience Managers** → Use AI chatbots to enhance support.
- **AI-Powered E-Commerce Consultants** → Automate online stores and advertising.

◈ **Action Plan:**

Find ways to **use AI to enhance your current job**, rather than waiting to be replaced.

3. Build Multiple AI-Driven Income Streams
◈ **Leverage AI to create passive income:**

- Sell **AI-generated ebooks, art, and digital products.**
- Automate **AI-powered freelancing and consulting services.**
- Start an **AI-driven online business or YouTube channel.**

◈ **Action Plan:**
Set up **at least one AI-powered income stream** in the next 30 days.

How AI is Enabling Entrepreneurs to Build Multimillion-Dollar Businesses

AI is **leveling the playing field for entrepreneurs**, allowing small business owners to **compete with billion-dollar companies**. AI-driven automation **reduces costs, scales operations, and increases efficiency**, making it easier than ever to **build a high-revenue company with minimal overhead**.

Step 1: Choose a Business Model That AI Can Automate

◈ **AI-Powered Business Ideas:**

◈ **AI Content Creation Agencies** → Use AI to generate blog posts, videos, and ad campaigns.

◈ **AI-Powered E-Commerce Stores** → Automate product research, customer service, and order fulfillment.

◈ **AI Chatbot & Automation Consulting** → Help businesses integrate AI-driven customer support.

◈ **AI Stock Trading & Financial Analysis** → Use AI to automate trading and investment strategies.

◈ **The key is to choose a business model where AI handles at least 80% of the workload!**

Step 2: Use AI to Automate Business Operations
◈ **AI-Driven Marketing & Sales Automation:**

- Use **ChatGPT & Jasper AI** to automate blog writing and social media content.
- Use **AdCreative AI** to generate Facebook & Google ads.
- Use **Zapier AI** to connect software and automate workflows.

◈ **AI-Driven Customer Service Automation:**

- Use **Tidio AI** or **ManyChat** to set up automated AI chatbots.
- Use **Drift AI** to **capture leads and book appointments automatically**.

◈ **AI-Driven Product Fulfillment & Logistics:**

- Use **Shopify AI & Printify AI** for **automated e-commerce fulfillment**.
- Use **AI-powered inventory management systems** to optimize stock levels.

◈ **By automating these key functions, you can scale your business to multimillion-dollar revenue without hiring a large team!**

Step 3: Scale with AI-Powered Growth Strategies
◈ **How to Scale an AI-Powered Business to $1M+ Revenue:**

- **Step 1:** Start with AI-automated content marketing (SEO, social media, and email marketing).
- **Step 2:** Use AI to optimize **advertising and customer acquisition**.
- **Step 3:** Scale with **AI-powered upsells, personalized product recommendations, and automation**.

◈ **Case Study: AI-Powered Print-on-Demand Business**

- **Uses AI to generate unique designs & automate production.**
- **Uses AI chatbots to handle customer inquiries.**
- **Uses AI-driven ad campaigns to attract new customers.**
- **Result:** Scales to **$100,000+ monthly revenue with a small team**.

Final Thoughts: The AI-Driven Future is Here—Are You Ready?

AI is **not just a trend—it's a complete transformation of the economy**. Those who **embrace AI and adapt quickly** will **thrive**, while those who resist will **fall behind**.

◈ **Key Takeaways for the Future of AI Jobs & Entrepreneurship:**
◈ AI will **replace repetitive jobs**, but **create high-paying, AI-enhanced careers**.
◈ Entrepreneurs can **build million-dollar businesses with minimal overhead** by using AI.

◈ Those who **learn AI skills and automation NOW** will be **leaders in the AI-driven economy**.

◈ **The Future Belongs to Those Who Use AI to Their Advantage.**

Are you ready to **profit from the AI revolution**? The time to act is **NOW**. ◈

Appendix A: AI Business Resources and Tools

As AI continues to revolutionize the way businesses operate, having access to the right tools and resources can make the difference between **stagnation and exponential growth**. Whether you are an entrepreneur, freelancer, content creator, or investor, leveraging AI-powered tools can help you **automate tasks, increase efficiency, and scale your income faster than ever before**.

This appendix serves as a **comprehensive guide to the best AI tools and resources** available for business owners and professionals who want to **maximize profits, automate operations, and stay ahead in the AI-driven economy**.

I. AI Tools for Content Creation and Marketing

1. AI Writing and Copywriting Tools

These tools help **automate blog writing, copywriting, ad campaigns, and social media posts**.

� **ChatGPT (OpenAI)** – AI-powered chatbot for content creation, automation, and research.

� https://openai.com/chatgpt

� **Jasper AI** – AI-driven writing assistant for blog posts, ad copy, and social media content.

� https://www.jasper.ai

� **Copy.ai** – AI tool for email copywriting, sales pages, and website content.

� https://www.copy.ai

� **SurferSEO** – AI-powered SEO tool for optimizing website content for search engines.

� https://www.surferseo.com

� **Best for:** Freelancers, bloggers, digital marketers, and business owners who want **high-quality AI-generated content**.

2. AI Tools for Graphic Design & Branding

These tools allow **non-designers to create professional-quality graphics and logos**.

◈ **Canva AI** – AI-powered design tool for social media graphics, logos, and presentations.
◈ https://www.canva.com

◈ **Midjourney** – AI art generator for creating digital artwork and branding materials.
◈ https://www.midjourney.com

◈ **DALL·E 3 (OpenAI)** – AI image generation tool for creating illustrations and graphics.
◈ https://openai.com/dall-e

◈ **Looka** – AI logo generator for branding and startup businesses.
◈ https://www.looka.com

◈ **Best for:** Freelance designers, e-commerce owners, and entrepreneurs who need **affordable, high-quality designs**.

3. AI Video Creation and Editing Tools

These tools help automate **video production, animation, and editing** for content creators.

◈ **Runway ML** – AI-powered video editing, special effects, and green screen removal.
◈ https://runwayml.com

◈ **Synthesia** – AI avatar and voiceover generator for corporate videos and e-learning.
◈ https://www.synthesia.io

◈ **Pictory AI** – AI tool for turning blog posts into **fully automated video content**.
◈ https://pictory.ai

◈ **Best for:** YouTubers, content creators, and businesses **looking to automate video production**.

II. AI Tools for E-Commerce & Sales Automation

4. AI-Powered E-Commerce Platforms

These tools allow **entrepreneurs to build online stores that run on autopilot**.

◈ **Shopify AI** – AI-powered e-commerce platform for dropshipping and print-on-demand.

◈ https://www.shopify.com

◈ **Printify AI** – AI-driven print-on-demand platform for selling custom products.

◈ https://www.printify.com

◈ **Sell The Trend** – AI-powered product research tool for finding trending e-commerce products.

◈ https://www.sellthetrend.com

◈ **Best for:** Dropshippers, print-on-demand entrepreneurs, and e-commerce business owners.

5. AI Chatbots & Customer Service Automation

These AI chatbots **automate customer support and sales inquiries**, reducing overhead costs.

◈ **ManyChat** – AI-powered chatbot for Facebook Messenger and WhatsApp automation.

◈ https://manychat.com

◈ **Tidio AI** – AI chatbot for automating customer service and lead generation.

◈ https://www.tidio.com

◈ **Drift AI** – AI chatbot for sales and customer engagement automation.

◈ https://www.drift.com

◈ **Best for:** Entrepreneurs who want to **automate sales and customer service without hiring a team**.

III. AI Tools for Business & Productivity

6. AI-Powered Productivity & Automation Tools

These tools help **businesses streamline operations and automate tasks**.

◈ **Zapier AI** – Automates workflows by integrating different AI tools and business apps.

◈ https://zapier.com

◈ **Notion AI** – AI-powered note-taking and project management platform.

◈ https://www.notion.so

◈ **Calendly AI** – AI-powered scheduling tool for booking meetings automatically.

◈ https://www.calendly.com

◈ **Best for:** Solopreneurs and teams **looking to streamline their workflows and eliminate manual tasks**.

IV. AI Tools for Investing & Finance

7. AI-Driven Stock & Crypto Trading

These tools use AI to **analyze market trends and automate trading decisions**.

◈ **Trade Ideas** – AI-powered stock trading platform for active investors.
◈ https://www.trade-ideas.com

◈ **3Commas** – AI-powered cryptocurrency trading bot for automated investing.
◈ https://3commas.io

◈ **Numerai** – AI-driven hedge fund that crowdsources predictive stock models.
◈ https://numer.ai

◈ **Best for:** Investors who want to **use AI for stock market and crypto trading automation**.

V. AI Tools for Passive Income & Digital Products

8. AI Tools for Passive Income Businesses

These AI-driven tools allow **entrepreneurs to create passive income streams**.

◈ **Gumroad** – AI-powered platform for selling digital products and memberships.
◈ https://www.gumroad.com

◈ **Teachable AI** – AI-assisted course creation platform for selling online courses.
◈ https://www.teachable.com

◈ **Koji AI** – AI-powered platform for selling digital content via social media.
◈ https://withkoji.com

◈ **Best for:** Anyone who wants to **sell AI-generated ebooks, courses, or digital templates**.

Final Thoughts: AI is the Future of Business

The right **AI tools can transform the way businesses operate, automate income, and scale to seven-figure revenues** with minimal overhead. Whether you are a **freelancer, entrepreneur, or investor**, adopting AI-driven strategies now will give you **a major competitive edge** in the coming years.

◈ **The key to success? Start using AI today and build a future-proof business!**

<u>Message from the Author</u>:

I hope you enjoyed this book, I love astrology and knew there was not a book such as this out on the shelf. I love metaphysical items as well. Please check out my other books:

-Life of Government Benefits

-My life of Hell

-My life with Hydrocephalus

-Red Sky

-World Domination:Woman's rule

-World Domination:Woman's Rule 2: The War

-Life and Banishment of Apophis: book 1

-The Kidney Friendly Diet

-The Ultimate Hemp Cookbook

-Creating a Dispensary(legally)

-Cleanliness throughout life: the importance of showering from childhood to adulthood.

-Strong Roots: The Risks of Overcoddling children

-Hemp Horoscopes: Cosmic Insights and Earthly Healing

- Celestial Hemp Navigating the Zodiac: Through the Green Cosmos

-Astrological Hemp: Aligning The Stars with Earth's Ancient Herb

-The Astrological Guide to Hemp: Stars, Signs, and Sacred Leaves

-Green Growth: Innovative Marketing Strategies for your Hemp Products and Dispensary

-Cosmic Cannabis

-Astrological Munchies

-Henry The Hemp

-Zodiacal Roots: The Astrological Soul Of Hemp

- **Green Constellations: Intersection of Hemp and Zodiac**

-Hemp in The Houses: An astrological Adventure Through The Cannabis Galaxy

-Galactic Ganja Guide

Heavenly Hemp

Zodiac Leaves

Doctor Who Astrology

Cannastrology

Stellar Satvias and Cosmic Indicas

Celestial Cannabis: A Zodiac Journey

AstroHerbology: The Sky and The Soil: Volume 1

AstroHerbology:Celestial Cannabis:Volume 2

Cosmic Cannabis Cultivation

The Starry Guide to Herbal Harmony: Volume 1

The Starry Guide to Herbal Harmony: Cannabis Universe: Volume 2

Yugioh Astrology: Astrological Guide to Deck, Duels and more

Nightmare Mansion: Echoes of The Abyss

Nightmare Mansion 2: Legacy of Shadows

Nightmare Mansion 3: Shadows of the Forgotten

Nightmare Mansion 4: Echoes of the Damned

The Life and Banishment of Apophis: Book 2

Nightmare Mansion: Halls of Despair

Healing with Herb: Cannabis and Hydrocephalus

Planetary Pot: Aligning with Astrological Herbs: Volume 1

Fast Track to Freedom: 30 Days to Financial Independence Using AI, Assets, and Agile Hustles

Cosmic Hemp Pathways

How to Become Financially Free in 30 Days: 10,000 Paths to Prosperity

Zodiacal Herbage: Astrological Insights: Volume 1

Nightmare Mansion: Whispers in the Walls

The Daleks Invade Atlantis

Henry the hemp and Hydrocephalus

10X The Kidney Friendly Diet

Cannabis Universe: Adult coloring book

Hemp Astrology: The Healing Power of the Stars

Zodiacal Herbage: Astrological Insights: Cannabis Universe: Volume 2

Planetary Pot: Aligning with Astrological Herbs: Cannabis Universes: Volume 2

Doctor Who Meets the Replicators and SG-1: The Ultimate Battle for Survival

Nightmare Mansion: Curse of the Blood Moon

The Celestial Stoner: A Guide to the Zodiac

Cosmic Pleasures: Sex Toy Astrology for Every Sign

Hydrocephalus Astrology: Navigating the Stars and Healing Waters

Lapis and the Mischievous Chocolate Bar

Celestial Positions: Sexual Astrology for Every Sign

Apophis's Shadow Work Journal: **:** A Journey of Self-Discovery and Healing

Kinky Cosmos: Sexual Kink Astrology for Every Sign

Digital Cosmos: The Astrological Digimon Compendium

Stellar Seeds: The Cosmic Guide to Growing with Astrology

Apophis's Daily Gratitude Journal

Cat Astrology: Feline Mysteries of the Cosmos

The Cosmic Kama Sutra: An Astrological Guide to Sexual Positions

Unleash Your Potential: A Guided Journal Powered by AI Insights

Whispers of the Enchanted Grove

Cosmic Pleasures: An Astrological Guide to Sexual Kinks

369, 12 Manifestation Journal

Whisper of the nocturne journal(blank journal for writing or drawing)

The Boogey Book

Locked In Reflection: A Chastity Journey Through Locktober

Generating Wealth Quickly:How to Generate $100,000 in 24 Hours

Star Magic: Harness the Power of the Universe

The Flatulence Chronicles: A Fart Journal for Self-Discovery

The Doctor and The Death Moth

Seize the Day: A Personal Seizure Tracking Journal

The Ultimate Boogeyman Safari: A Journey into the Boogie World and Beyond

Whispers of Samhain: 1,000 Spells of Love, Luck, and Lunar Magic: Samhain Spell Book

Apophis's guides:Witch's Spellbook Crafting Guide for Halloween

Frost & Flame: The Enchanted Yule Grimoire of 1000 Winter Spells

The Ultimate Boogey Goo Guide & Spooky Activities for Halloween Fun

Harmony of the Scales: A Libra's Spellcraft for Balance and Beauty

The Enchanted Advent: 36 Days of Christmas Wonders

Nightmare Mansion: The Labyrinth of Screams

Harvest of Enchantment: 1,000 Spells of Gratitude, Love, and Fortune for Thanksgiving

The Boogey Chronicles: A Journal of Nightly Encounters and Shadowy Secrets

The 12 Days of Financial Freedom: A Step-by-Step Christmas Countdown to Transform Your Finances

Sigil of the Eternal Spiral Blank Journal

A Christmas Feast: Timeless Recipes for Every Meal

Holiday Stress-Free Solutions: A Survival Guide to Thriving During the Festive Season

Yu-Gi-Oh! Holiday Gifting Mastery: The Ultimate Guide for Fans and Newcomers Alike

Holiday Harmony: A Hydrocephalus Survival Guide for the Festive Season

Celestial Craft: The Witch's Almanac for 2025 – A Cosmic Guide to Manifestations, Moons, and Mystical Events

Doctor Who: The Toymaker's Winter Wonderland

Tulsa King Unveiled: A Thrilling Guide to Stallone's Mafia Masterpiece

Pendulum Craft: A Complete Guide to Crafting and Using Personalized Divination Tools

Nightmare Mansion: Santa's Eternal Eve

Starlight Noel: A Cosmic Journey through Christmas Mysteries

The Dark Architect: Unlocking the Blueprint of Existence

Surviving the Embrace: The Ultimate Guide to Encounters with The Hugging Molly

The Enchanted Codex: Secrets of the Craft for Witches, Wiccans, and Pagans

Harvest of Gratitude: A Complete Thanksgiving Guide

Yuletide Essentials: A Complete Guide to an Authentic and Magical Christmas

Celestial Smokes: A Cosmic Guide to Cigars and Astrology

Living in Balance: A Comprehensive Survival Guide to Thriving with Diabetes Insipidus

Cosmic Symbiosis: The Venom Zodiac Chronicles

The Cursed Paw of Ambition

Cosmic Symbiosis: The Astrological Venom Journal

Celestial Wonders Unfold: A Stargazer's Guide to the Cosmos (2024-2029)

The Ultimate Black Friday Prepper's Guide: Mastering Shopping Strategies and Savings

Cosmic Sales: The Astrological Guide to Black Friday Shopping

Legends of the Corn Mother and Other Harvest Myths

Whispers of the Harvest: The Corn Mother's Journal

The Evergreen Spellbook

The Doctor Meets the Boogeyman

The White Witch of Rose Hall's SpellBook

The Gingerbread Golem's Shadow: A Study in Sweet Darkness

The Gingerbread Golem Codex: An Academic Exploration of Sweet Myths

The Gingerbread Golem Grimoire: Sweet Magicks and Spells for the Festive Witch

The Curse of the Gingerbread Golem

10-minute Christmas Crafts for kids

Christmas Crisis Solutions: The Ultimate Last-Minute Survival Guide

Gingerbread Golem Recipes: Holiday Treats with a Magical Twist

The Infinite Key: Unlocking Mystical Secrets of the Ages

Enchanted Yule: A Wiccan and Pagan Guide to a Magical and Memorable Season

Dinosaurs of Power: Unlocking Ancient Magick

Astro-Dinos: The Cosmic Guide to Prehistoric Wisdom

Gallifrey's Yule Logs: A Festive Doctor Who Cookbook

The Dino Grimoire: Secrets of Prehistoric Magick

The Gift They Never Knew They Needed

The Gingerbread Golem's Culinary Alchemy: Enchanting Recipes for a Sweetly Dark Feast

A Time Lord Christmas: Holiday Adventures with the Doctor

Krampusproofing Your Home: Defensive Strategies for Yule

Silent Frights: A Collection of Christmas Creepypastas to Chill Your Bones

Santa Raptor's Jolly Carnage: A Dino-Claus Christmas Tale

Prehistoric Palettes: A Dino Wicca Coloring Journey

The Christmas Wishkeeper Chronicles

The Starlight Sleigh: A Holiday Journey

Elf Secrets: The True Magic of the North Pole

Candy Cane Conjurations

Cooking with Kids: Recipes Under 20 Minutes

Doctor Who: The TARDIS Confiscation

The Anxiety First Aid Kit: Quick Tools to Calm Your Mind

Frosty Whispers: A Winter's Tale

The Infinite Key: Unlocking the Secrets to Prosperity, Resilience, and Purpose

The Grasping Void: Why You'll Regret This Purchase

Astrology for Busy Bees: Star Signs Simplified

The Instant Focus Formula: Cut Through the Noise

The Secret Language of Colors: Unlocking the Emotional Codes

Sacred Fossil Chronicles: Blank Journal

The Christmas Cottage Miracle

Feeding Frenzy: Graboid-Inspired Recipes

Manifest in Minutes: The Quick Law of Attraction Guide

The Symbiote Chronicles: Doctor Who's Venomous Journey

Think Tiny, Grow Big: The Minimalist Mindset

The Energy Key: Unlocking Limitless Motivation

New Year, New Magic: Manifesting Your Best Year Yet

Unstoppable You: Mastering Confidence in Minutes

Infinite Energy: The Secret to Never Feeling Drained

Lightning Focus: Mastering the Art of Productivity in a Distracted World

Saturnalia Manifestation Magick: A Guide to Unlocking Abundance During the Solstice

Graboids and Garland: The Ultimate Tremors-Themed Christmas Guide

12 Nights of Holiday Magic

The Power of Pause: 60-Second Mindfulness Practices

The Quick Reset: How to Reclaim Your Life After Burnout

The Shadow Eater: A Tale of Despair and Survival

The Micro-Mastery Method: Transform Your Skills in Just Minutes a Day

Reclaiming Time: How to Live More by Doing Less

Chronovore: The Eternal Nexus

The Mind Reset: Unlocking Your Inner Peace in a Chaotic World
Confidence Code: Building Unshakable Self-Belief
Baby the Vampire Terrier
Baby the Vampire Terrier's Christmas Adventure
Celestial Streams: The Content Creator's Astrology Manual
The Wealth Whisperer: Unlocking Abundance with Everyday Actions
The Energy Equation: Maximize Your Output Without Burning Out
The Happiness Algorithm: Science-Backed Steps to Joyful Living
Stress-Free Success: Achieving Goals Without Anxiety
Mindful Wealth: The New Blueprint for Financial Freedom
The Festive Flavors of New Year: A Culinary Celebration
The Master's Gambit: Keys of Eternal Power
Shadowed Secrets: Groundhog Day Mysteries
Beneath the Burrow: Lessons from the Groundhog
Spring's Whispers: The Groundhog's Prediction
The Limitless Mindset: Unlock Your Untapped Potential
The Focus Funnel: How to Cut Through Chaos and Get Results
Bold Moves: Building Courage to Live on Your Terms
The Daily Shift: Simple Practices for Lasting Transformation
The Quarter-Life Reset: Thriving in Your 20s and 30s
The Art of Shadowplay: Building Your Own Personal Myth
The Eternal Loop: Finding Purpose in Repetition
Burrowing Wisdom: Life Lessons from the Groundhog
Shadow Work: A Groundhog Day Perspective
Love in Bloom: 5-Minute Romantic Gestures
The Shadowspell Codex: Secrets of Forbidden Magick
The Burnout Cure: Finding Balance in a Busy World
The Groundhog Prophecy: Unlocking Seasonal Secrets
Nog Tales: The Spirited History of Eggnog
Six More Weeks: Embracing Seasonal Transitions
The Lumivian Chronicles: Fragments of the Fifth Dimension

Money on Your Mind: A Beginner's Guide to Wealth
The Focus Fix: Breaking Through Distraction
January's Spirit Keepers: Mystical Protectors of the Cold
Creativity Unchained: Unlocking Your Wildest Ideas in 2025
Manifestation Mastery: 365 Days to Rewrite Your Reality
The Groundhog's Mirror: Reflecting on Change
The Weeping Angels' Christmas Curse
Burrowed in Time: A Groundhog Day Journey
Heartbeats: Poems to Share with Your Valentine
Dino Wicca: The Sacred Grimoire of Prehistoric Magick
Courage of the Pride: Finding Your Inner Roar
The Lion's Leap: Bold Moves for Big Results
Healthy Hustle: Achieving Without Overworking
Practical Manifesting: Turning Dreams into Reality in 2025
Jurassic Pharaohs: Unlocking the Magick of Ancient Egypt and Dino Wicca
The Happiness Equation: Small Changes for Big Joy
The Confidence Compass: Finding Your Inner Strength
Whispers in the Hollow: Tales of the Forgotten Beasts
Echoes from the Hollow: The Return of Forgotten Beasts
The Hollow Ascendant: The Rise of the Forgotten Beasts
The Relationship Reset: Building Better Connections
Mastering the Morning: How to Win the Day Before 8 AM
The Shadow's Dance: Groundhog Day Symbolism
Cupid's Kitchen: Quick Valentine's Day Recipes
Valentine's Day on a Budget: Love Without Breaking the Bank
Astrocraft: Aligning the Stars in the World of Minecraft
Forecasting Life: Groundhog Day Reflections

Bleeding Hearts: Twisted Tales of Valentine's Terror

Herbal Smoke Revolution: The Ultimate Guide to Nature's Cigarette Alternative

Winter's Wrath: The Complete Survival Blueprint for Extreme Freezes.

The Groundhog's Shadow: A Tale of Seasons
Burrowed Insights: Wisdom from the Groundhog
Sensual Strings: The Art of Erotic Bondage
Whispered Flames: Unlocking the Power of Fire Play
Forgotten Shadows: A Guide to Cryptids Lost to Time
Six Weeks of Secrets: Groundhog Day's Hidden Messages
Shadows and Cycles: Groundhog Day Reflections
The Art of Love Letters: Crafting the Perfect Message
Romantic Getaways at Home: Turning Your Space into Paradise
Purrfect Brews: A Cat Lover's Guide to Coffee and Companionship
The Groundhog's Wisdom: Timeless Lessons for Modern Life
The Shadow Oracle: Groundhog Day as a Predictor
Emerging from the Burrow: A Journey of Renewal
The Language of Love: Learning Your Partner's Love Style
Authorpreneur: The Ultimate Blueprint for Writing, Publishing, and Thriving as an Author
Weathering the Seasons: Groundhog Day Perspectives
Valentine's Day Magic: A Guide to Romantic Rituals
The Shadow Chronicles: Stories of Groundhog Day
Love and Laughter: Fun Games for Valentine's Day
AstroRealty: Unlocking the Stars for Property Success
The Groundhog's Path: A Guide to Seasonal Balance
Groundhog Day Diaries: Reflections in the Shadow
The Groundhog's Light: Illuminating the Path Ahead
Valentine's Traditions from Around the World
AI Wealth Revolution: Unlocking the Trillionaire Mindset
Love Rekindled: Reigniting Passion in Relationships
Single and Thriving: Self-Love on Valentine's Day
Emerald Legends: Mystical Tales of Ireland
Green Alchemy: Harnessing Nature's Magic
The Hearts of Horror: A Valentine's Day Nightmare

The Leprechaun's Guide to Wealth and Wisdom

Dancing with the Sidhe: Celebrating the Otherworld

Shamrocks and Shadows: Mysteries of the Green Isle

Emerald Energy: Harnessing Luck and Growth

The Gingerbread Golem's Valentine: A Sweetheart's Guide to Love and Enchantment

The Celtic Knot: Weaving Life and Destiny

Green Fire: Elemental Magic for St. Patrick's Day

Clover Chronicles: Finding Your Inner Luck

Ireland's Mystical Creatures: A Field Guide

Gingerbread Golem's Love Almanac

Prowl and Thrive: The Lion's Guide to Success

Love Alchemy: Transforming Your Life Through Heart Energy

WORLD DOMINATION: Woman's Rule 3:The New Life

The Midnight Rose: A Guide to Lunar Love Spells

The Forbidden Letters: Writing Your Own Love Prophecy

Luck and Lore: St. Patrick's Day for Modern Mystics

The Green Path: A Pagan Celebration of Renewal

The Dark Architect's Guide to Reprogramming Reality

Prankster's Paradise: A Guide to Harmless Hijinks

Manifest Your Reality: The Law of Attraction Simplified

The TARDIS Owner's Manual: Understanding the Doctor's Ship: *A complete guide to the TARDIS, its technology, secrets, and mysteries*

Starlit Romance: Astrology Secrets for Finding True Love

The Time Lord's Atlas: A Complete Guide to the Whoniverse: ***A breakdown of the locations, planets, and dimensions explored in Doctor Who***

Sweetheart Shadows: The Dark Side of Love and Attraction

February Fire: Reigniting Passion in Every Area of Life

The Self-Love Toolkit: 5 Ways to Embrace Who You Are

February Sparks: Ignite Your Dreams in 28 Days

March to Success: A 31-Day Action Blueprint
Ancient Paths: The 13 Sacred Principles of Dino Wicca
Echoes of Tomorrow: Navigating the AI Revolution
The Wellness Blueprint: Balancing Mind, Body, and Soul
Green Horizons: Sustainable Living for a Better Tomorrow
The AI Wealth Code: How to Make Millions with Automation
AI-Powered Creativity: Writing, Art, and Music for Profit
Extinction Rites: Rebirthing Your Soul Through Prehistoric Magick
Sacred Serpents tarot
Celestial Enchantment blank journal
Star Strains
Culinary Journeys: Exploring Global Flavors at Home
The Hollowvale Curse
The Hollowvale Harvest
The Egg of Transformation: Awakening Your Inner Power
Blooming Into Power: A Wiccan Guide to Spring Awakening
The Nightmare Nexus: The Third Doctor's Perilous Haunting
Digital Detox: Reclaiming Your Life in a Connected World
Ostara's Path: Walking the Spiral of Renewal
The Sacred Hare
Financial Freedom: Building Wealth in the Modern Age
Spring's Cauldron: Stirring the Waters of Change
The Hollowvale Pact
Quantum Consciousness: The Science of Reality Shifting
The Hollowvale Hunger
The Sacred Waters Within: A Witch's Guide to Hydrocephalus Magick
The Raven's Nest: Building a Life of Unshakable Stability
AI and the Human Mind: The Future of Intelligence
The Hollowvale Reckoning
Timeless Love: Building and Maintaining Lasting Relationships

The Raven's Roar: Unlocking Unstoppable Confidence
Raven Sight: Awakening Intuition and Inner Wisdom
The Butterfly Effect: Small Changes, Big Transformations
Taming the Boogeyman: How to Conquer Your Inner Fears
The Magick of Green: Awakening Earth's Energy in You
The Entrepreneurial Mindset: Secrets to Business Success
The Hollowvale End
The Shadow Luck Ritual: Reclaiming Power from Your Dark Side
Spring Magick for Beginners: A Simple Guide to Seasonal Energy Work
Doctor Who: The Hollowvale Conundrum
The March of Miracles: Unlocking Synchronicities in Spring
Unveiling the Cosmos: A Guide to Stargazing and Space Exploration
The Ultimate Guide to Surviving an Economic Collapse

If you want solar for your home go here: https://www.harborsolar.live/apophisenterprises/

Get Some Tarot cards: https://www.makeplayingcards.com/sell/apophis-occult-shop

Get some shirts: https://www.bonfire.com/store/apophis-shirt-emporium/

Instagrams:
@apophis_enterprises,
@apophisbookemporium,
@apophisscardshop
Twitter: @apophisenterpr1
Tiktok:@apophisenterprise
Youtube: @sg1fan23477, @FiresideRetreatKingdom
Hive: @sg1fan23477
CheeLee: @SG1fan23477

Podcast: Apophis Chat Zone: https://open.spotify.com/show/5zXbrCLEV2xzCp8ybrfHsk?si=fb4d4fdbdce44dec

Newsletter: https://apophiss-newsletter-27c897.beehiiv.com/

If you want to support me or see posts of other projects that I have come over to: **buymeacoffee.com/mpetchinskg**

I post there daily several times a day

Get your Dinowicca or Christmas themed digital products, especially Santa Raptor songs and other musics. Here: **https://sg1fan23477.gumroad.com**

Apophis Yuletide Digital has not only digital Christmas items, but it will have all things with Dinowicca as well as other Digital products.

www.ingramcontent.com/pod-product-compliance
Lightning Source LLC
LaVergne TN
LVHW022008200926
848481LV00007B/2286
* 9 7 9 8 3 4 8 5 8 6 9 9 7 *